IMAGES
of America

FLORENCE

IMAGES
of America

FLORENCE

Carolyn Barske

ARCADIA
PUBLISHING

Published by Arcadia Publishing
Charleston, South Carolina

Library of Congress Control Number: 2013955179

For all general information, please contact Arcadia Publishing:
Telephone 843-853-2070
Fax 843-853-0044
E-mail sales@arcadiapublishing.com
For customer service and orders:
Toll-Free 1-888-313-2665

Visit us on the Internet at www.arcadiapublishing.com

To Billy Warren, whose love for historic preservation and the history of his hometown has inspired me since the first day we met—Florence is very lucky to have such a wonderful person on its side.

CONTENTS

ACKNOWLEDGMENTS

Many people have worked very hard to bring this book together. Graduate students Clint Alley, Jesse Brock, and Wesley Garmon, who are all part of the University of North Alabama Public History graduate program, did the bulk of the scanning, research, and photography when we could not find historical images of important places in and around Florence. Without their hard work, this book would not have been possible.

I would also like to thank Louise Huddleston, the archivist at the Collier Library Archives and Special Collections at the University of North Alabama, for her hard work and patience as this project has gone forward. A thank-you goes to Judy Sizemore, director of the Muscle Shoals National Heritage Area, for her advice and participation in the project. Nancy Sanford, the director of the Florence-Lauderdale Public Library, graciously allowed access to the library's digital archives and also allowed her employees to assist in this project. A thank-you is also given to Lee Freeman of the Florence-Lauderdale Public Library for all of the information he shared with us about Florence. Thanks go to Florence Main Street for its help on this project and for letting us use images from its annual calendars. I would also like to give thanks to Falon Yates for her help with the photography. And a big thank-you is owed to Vince Brewton for sending this project my way.

I would also like to thank Jesse Darland, Lydia Rollins, and Jason Humphrey of Arcadia Publishing for all of their help during this process.

The images in this volume appear courtesy of the University of North Alabama Collier Library Archives and Special Collections (UNA), the Florence Lauderdale Public Library (FLPL), and Florence Main Street (FMS).

INTRODUCTION

On March 12, 1818, members of the Cypress Land Company met in Huntsville, Alabama, to determine the exact location of a new city on the Tennessee River in Northwest Alabama. The area that would become Florence was familiar to some of the members of the Cypress Land Company already, including Gens. John Coffee and Andrew Jackson; they had met in Northwest Alabama to survey potential locations in 1817. In fact, Jackson's Military Road, which ran from Nashville to New Orleans, went right through the area that would become Florence. Once the Cypress Land Company determined the exact location, General Coffee worked with a young Italian surveyor, Ferdinand Sannoner, to lay out the city of Florence. The original plan included space for a college, a female seminary, and a public walk. The company held the first land sale on July 22, 1818. With 52 lots sold, the company had grossed nearly $225,000 shortly after the Panic of 1819 hit, which slowed sales of town lots dramatically. However, by 1821, the economy was on the road to recovery, and another land sale was held that led to a building boom across the town. Florence was well on its way to becoming an established community and a successful investment for those who had taken the risk and purchased land. Members of the Cypress Land Company, including Irish immigrant James Jackson, future Supreme Court justice John McKinley, and Gen. John Coffee, made their homes in Florence and worked hard to ensure their vision flourished.

Behind this success story is a much sadder tale. The establishment of the city of Florence in 1818 was only possible because of the secession of Native American lands to the US government. In 1816, the Chickasaw Nation ceded its lands north of the Tennessee River, followed by the Cherokee in 1817. Explorers had long noted the area for its rich soil and abundant natural resources. When lands in the East increasingly became worn out because of poor farming practices, it was only logical that farmers and plantation owners would look westward. At first, white settlers pushed into the area illegally, squatting on Native American lands. The opening of the Natchez Trace in 1803 as a post road spurred the growth of more illegal settlements on both sides of the Tennessee River. By 1810, thousands of settlers lived on Chickasaw lands. The US government initially tried to remove the squatters. However, by the time of the land secessions in 1816 and 1817, it was clear to all parties that white settlement of the area was inevitable. To make room for white settlers, Native Americans were moved onto reservations in the Tennessee River valley region. This was only the first step toward the huge wave of Native American removal that would come in the 1830s after the passage of President Jackson's Indian Removal Act of 1830.

What made the men of the Cypress Land Company choose Florence as the site of their new community? Florence sits at the base of the once-formidable Muscle Shoals (also historically spelled Mussel Shoals). The shoals, which ran for about 40 miles, with an average drop of 3.5 feet per mile, made travel along the full length of the Tennessee River extremely difficult. Many realized that if the shoals could be tamed, the area would flourish. Even before official settlement began, there was discussion about the necessity of making the shoals navigable.

In 1805, the Tennessee State Legislature asked the US Congress to open the Muscle Shoals. However, it would not be until 1836 that a canal spanning the Big Muscle Shoals opened, and even then, the canal, with its 17 locks, did not even come close to solving the problem, as it did not span the Elk River Shoals or the Little Muscle Shoals. Regardless of the problems posed by the shoals, the location of Florence on the river would be beneficial for river trade moving westward. The site chosen for Florence sat 100 feet above the river, which many saw as a health benefit, as low-lying areas were thought to be more disease-prone. The river valley's rich soil was an obvious draw, and the area's climate allowed for the production of both wheat and cotton. The numerous creeks that fed into the Tennessee River created ideal spots for the construction of factories and mills. Abundant natural resources, including iron ore, stone, coal, and timber also made Florence the logical choice to the members of the Cypress Creek Land Company.

The development of the city of Florence began rapidly. Within a year of the first land sale, the city had its first newspaper, the *Florence Weekly Gazette*. Brick buildings and frame houses lined the streets of the city within a few years of its founding, which was atypical for a frontier town in the early 19th century. By 1820, the population of Lauderdale County, of which Florence was the county seat, was 4,693 (3,556 white residents, 1,407 free and enslaved black residents). Schools for both boys and girls began to open, churches were built, and by 1840, the first railroad and traffic bridge across the Tennessee River opened. In 1855, LaGrange College moved to Florence from its previous location in Leighton, Alabama. In 1830, LaGrange College had been the first institution of higher education to be chartered by the State of Alabama. The school's name was changed to Florence Wesleyan University after the move. The school, which today is named the University of North Alabama (UNA), has played an important role in the growth of Florence and in the educational history of Alabama.

By the outbreak of the Civil War in 1861, Florence was a thriving community. Sawmills, gristmills, tanneries, brick factories, gun factories, and flour mills dotted the shore of the river and the numerous creeks that fed into it. The Globe Factory, the largest textile mill in Alabama before the Civil War, was located in Florence and employed more than 300 workers. The city had become a shipping point for liquor firms, as well as a cotton center. However, when the war struck Florence, life changed dramatically. Though no major battles were fought in Florence, the city changed hands over 40 times during the war. Well-known generals from both sides spent time in Florence, including William Tecumseh Sherman, Nathan Bedford Forrest, and John Bell Hood. Both Union and Confederate forces were responsible for widespread destruction of property in and around Florence, normally to keep the other side from gaining access to supplies. Confederate forces destroyed the railroad bridge that spanned the Tennessee River in order to prevent the Union forces from using it. Union and Confederate forces also damaged many of the mills and factories located along the river. By the end of the war in 1865, both the economy and infrastructure of Florence were largely ruined.

It was not until 1875, when the second phase of canal-building began on the Tennessee River, that Florence began to recover from the devastation wrought by the war. By the mid-1880s, an industrial boom largely centered in East Florence brought growth and economic recovery to the area. In 1886, the Florence Land, Mining and Manufacturing Company purchased land in East Florence, and in 1887, the North Alabama Furnace, Foundry and Land Company opened. One of the largest and most successful companies in Florence, the Florence Wagon Works, relocated from Atlanta to Florence in 1889 to take advantage of the cheap transportation provided by the Tennessee River and the plentiful hardwood that could be harvested around Florence. Florence Wagon Works would go on to become the second-largest producer of wagons in the United States behind Studebaker. In 1893, Cherry Cotton Mills relocated from Barton, Alabama, and in 1899, the Ashcraft Cotton Mill opened. In the early 1900s, the Tennessee Valley Fertilizer Company, International Mineral Corporation, and Coleman Cotton Gin and Cleaner Works all opened their doors in Florence. At the height of the boom years, over 50 corporations operated in East Florence. The population of Florence grew along with industry, reaching 6,000 in 1889. By the time that the new shoals canal opened in 1890, Florence was well on its way to becoming an industrial center in North Alabama.

As growth continued, the question of how best to tame the Tennessee River continued to occupy many residents' minds. The canal had helped solve some of the navigation problems that had plagued the city since its founding, but the river still destroyed millions of dollars of property every time it flooded. If the river could be tamed, it would not only prevent such wanton destruction of property, but it could also generate power to help to fuel industrial development on both sides of the river. However, it was not until World War I began that any plans came together to build such a dam. The need for synthetic nitrates for the war effort pushed leaders in Washington to select the area for the development of two nitrate factories, to be powered by what would become the Wilson Dam. In August 1918, construction of the two nitrate plants began across the river from Florence in Sheffield and on the Wilson Dam Reservation. Villages were built to house the future workers. Construction of the dam did not begin until November 8, just three days before the armistice was signed. Despite the war's end, plans for the dam went forward. The project, which employed over 4,000 workers, took six years to complete. At 137 feet tall and 4,535 feet long, the Wilson Dam was the largest dam in the world when it was completed on September 12, 1925. The two locks opened on June 1, 1927.

Serious questions emerged during the construction of the dam about the future of the project. With the war over, the need for synthetic nitrates decreased dramatically. To what use should the dam and the factories be put? Even before the dam was completed in 1921, Henry Ford made an offer of $5 million for the purchase of the nitrate plants, and he also proposed leasing the dam upon its completion for $1.7 million. He would produce fertilizer using the plants, but he also proposed developing the 75-mile stretch between Florence and Huntsville into an industrial center. Despite the fact that many in the Shoals community were excited about the possibility of Ford developing the region, others were not so sure. More than $130 million in taxpayer money had been spent on the dam and the nitrate plants, and some people, like Sen. George Norris of Nebraska, thought that the Tennessee River should be developed as a resource for the people of the region. He and others worried that Ford's plan would focus too heavily on the industrial side of the coin and neglect navigation, forestry, and agriculture. In the end, Ford withdrew his proposal, and the fate of the Wilson Dam remained up in the air until the Great Depression struck.

In 1932, in the deepest depths of the Great Depression, more than a quarter of Florence residents were unemployed. A Hooverville had sprung up along the railroad line. Little aid from the Hoover Administration ever reached Florence. Instead, community organizations helped those who suffered the most, though quickly these groups found their resources taxed. Cotton prices fell dramatically, and food supplies became scarce. The Tennessee River valley as a whole was one of the most depressed areas in the country, and Alabama was the hardest hit state in the South. However, in 1933, things began to change dramatically for the region. On January 21, president-elect Franklin Delano Roosevelt visited the Shoals and promised to turn the nitrate factories into fertilizer plants, which would become the centerpiece of the Tennessee Valley Authority (TVA). On May 18, 1933, TVA was formally created, and the fertilizer factories started up. A new ammonia plant was constructed and work began on Wheeler Dam, 16 miles north of Wilson Dam, on November 21, 1933. Construction of Pickwick Dam, located 52 miles below Wilson Dam, began on March 8, 1935. Florence residents found work on these and other New Deal projects in the Shoals region, including the construction of Willingham Hall on the campus of UNA by the Works Progress Administration (WPA), but others were forced to move to make way for the dams. Despite the negative effects on some residents, TVA dramatically changed the Shoals region as a whole, providing electricity, jobs, and fertilizer to people all along the river valley.

By the mid-20th century, Florence was once again a thriving community and remains so today. The University of North Alabama continues to occupy an important role in the community, providing educational opportunities, sponsoring cultural events, and serving as an intellectual center for North Alabama. The downtown storefronts are almost all full—a rarity in many smaller communities across the country. The Florence Main Street Program and Downtown Florence Unlimited have worked hard to keep the downtown this way, sponsoring "First Fridays" and other events to highlight downtown and local businesses. City museums help to tell the history of past Florence residents, including the Rosenbaum family and W.C. Handy, the "Father of the Blues." Community festivals, including the W.C. Handy Music Festival and the Alabama Renaissance Faire, draw people from across the country to Florence.

The images contained in this book help to tell the story of the people who have helped to make Florence into the busiest and largest city in Northwest Alabama. Many of the homes they built, the businesses they owned, the schools they supported, and the churches they attended are documented on the following pages. From its frontier roots to today, Florence has truly lived up to its nickname, "Alabama's Renaissance City."

One

THE CITY OF FLORENCE

This view of Court Street, before it was paved, shows that downtown has always been a busy place. Florence does not have a Main Street. Instead, Court Street is the heart of downtown. (UNA.)

This is a 1890 view of Tennessee Street, looking east from the intersection with Court Street. (FLPL.)

Early-20th-century Florence offered a wide variety of transportation options. The Tri-Cities trolley line was incorporated in 1904 and continued to serve the residents of the Shoals until the 1940s. This image shows the streetcar rails in Court Street, facing north toward what is today Rogers Hall on the campus of the University of North Alabama. (FLPL.)

The image above of Court Street, looking south toward the Tennessee River, shows the historic Rogers Department Store with the rotunda of Lauderdale County's second courthouse (1900–1965) soaring in the background. The image below shows Court Street looking north from Tennessee Street toward the campus of the University of North Alabama. (Both FLPL.)

This is an undated view of the corner of Tennessee and Court Streets, looking south. (FLPL.)

While much has changed in Florence since the 1920s, when these pictures were taken, many of the buildings shown here on Court Street still remain an integral part of downtown. (UNA.)

The image above of City Park from the turn of the 20th century includes the Elk's Home (at left) and the John McKinley Federal Building. When Ferdinand Sannoner developed the first plan for the city of Florence in 1818, he included an area designated as a public walk. The park contains a fountain, shown below, designed and constructed by the White Stone Company of Memphis, Tennessee. The Douglass family donated the fountain to the city, in the memory of James Josephus Douglass. Douglass built the Kennedy-Douglass house, which is now home to the Kennedy-Douglass Center for the Arts. Long known as Town Park, the name was changed in 1924 to Wilson Park, in honor of Pres. Woodrow Wilson. (Above, FLPL; below, FMS.)

This street scene from a residential neighborhood near the University of North Alabama was taken around 1911. The image clearly shows the architectural and aesthetic layout of Florence's downtown residential area at the turn of the 20th century. (FLPL.)

The Florence-Lauderdale Public Library was built to serve the needs of the area, which previously had only small reading rooms. In 1945, Louis Rosenbaum, the proprietor of a local chain of movie theaters, donated $25,000 to acquire or build a permanent home for the library. His son, Stanley, also contributed to the cause. On January 9, 1949, the Florence-Lauderdale Public Library opened its doors at 218 North Wood Avenue, where it stood until moving to its current location less than a block north on Wood Avenue in 2002. (UNA.)

One of Florence's hidden treasures is the 42-foot-high ancient mound that overlooks the Tennessee River on South Court Street. The founders of Florence laid out the city around the mound, as can be seen by its presence on the oldest surviving map of the town. The Florence mound is one of the largest surviving mounds in the region, likely built around 500 AD as a temple mound. (UNA.)

The current Florence Post Office shares a building with a federal courthouse, which was built on the site of the Old Presbyterian Female Synodical College. Much of the construction of the post office and federal courthouse was done with teams of mules, as can be seen in this image from February 1, 1912. (FLPL.)

James K. Taylor, cousin to Episcopal priest Hiram Kennedy-Douglass, designed the federal building. Taylor utilized both Alabama and Georgia marble in the construction of the Neoclassical structure. Soon after the building opened, a rumor began circulating that when the request for the new post office building was submitted for approval by the federal government, it was mixed up with a similar request from Florence, South Carolina, and somehow Florence, Alabama, got that city's plans. In 1913, Florence, Alabama, was a small town, while Florence, South Carolina, was a much larger community, and it did not make sense to many people that the smaller community was allowed to construct such a large building. However, the truth of the matter was that a senator who had more power than the South Carolina senator represented Florence, Alabama, in Congress. The building was, in fact, designed for Florence, Alabama. In 1998, the building was renamed to honor US Supreme Court Justice John McKinley, who was one of the founders of Florence. In 2012, the federal district courtroom on the third floor was restored to its original state through the work of Judge Inge Johnson. (UNA.)

Lauderdale County's first courthouse served as the seat of justice for Lauderdale County from 1821 to 1899. The unfinished base of the monument to Lauderdale County's Confederate veterans can be seen at the right. The monument was begun in the 1870s, but lack of funding and a desire to forget the horrors of war left it unfinished until the monument-building craze of the late 1890s and early 1900s renewed interest in memorializing the county's aging Confederate veterans. (FLPL.)

Lauderdale County's second courthouse was a large Neoclassical structure that sat on Court Street from 1900 to 1965. It occupied a spacious square one block north of the location of the third (current) courthouse. (UNA.)

The present Lauderdale County Courthouse was built in 1965. The modern style chosen for the building differs dramatically from that of its predecessors. The memorial to the Confederate veterans, seen unfinished in the image of the first courthouse, appears completed here. (FLPL.)

This picture of the electric car line was taken near the old Southern Railroad station in Florence. The line ran between Sheffield and Florence. (UNA.)

This is the first electric car of the Sheffield Company electric car line to cross the bridge of the Southern Railroad Company over the Tennessee River in 1904. (UNA.)

Not all public transportation in Florence was quite as commodious as the electric car line, as this early public transfer vehicle illustrates. This photograph may be associated with J.W. Paulk's Mule Barn, which was established in 1914 or 1915. The barn and adjoining livery stable, owned by Henry Aiken, was located at the corner of Tennessee Street and Wood Avenue. (UNA.)

The original centerpiece of the Tennessee Valley Authority's hydroelectric program, Wilson Dam was built by the US Army Corps of Engineers between 1918 and 1925. It is a concrete gravity dam on a blue limestone rock foundation, standing at an elevation of 508 feet. It is 4,535 feet long and 137 feet tall, with a maximum width of 160 feet. This photograph shows the construction of the dam. (FLPL.)

22

The Eliza Coffee Memorial Hospital was founded in 1919 (above). It was made possible in part by a donation of $10,000 from Camilla M. Coffee, who requested that the hospital be named in memory of her daughter, Eliza. Its first location, seen above, was on East Tuscaloosa Street, in a building that had originally been erected as an apartment building by the Florence Land Company. This apartment building had been used to help house the large numbers of people who came to town to work on Wilson Dam. A 1925 article from the *Florence Times* claims that the Tuscaloosa Street building boasted comfortable—albeit racially segregated—accommodations for 60 total patients. The hospital moved to its current facility, pictured below, on South Marengo Street in 1943. (Above, FLPL; below, UNA.)

After a big fire at the Florence passenger station on South Court Street, all railroad activities for Florence and Lauderdale County were conducted through the East Florence depot. In 1888, a spur had been built to serve the industrial center in East Florence. The Louisville & Nashville Railroad maintained both a passenger and freight depot in East Florence. (UNA.)

The Jackson Ford Bridge, also known as the Cypress Creek Bridge but best known as the Ghost Bridge, was built around 1912 and was named after Jackson Ford, which, itself was named after the James Jackson Sr. of the Forks of Cypress. The bridge was dismantled in 2013. According to tradition, the ghost of one of "Mountain" Tom Clark's victims haunted the bridge. (FLPL.)

Two

BUSINESSES

Texan Paul Trowbridge, who also later opened the Dixie Dairy plant on Seminary Street, founded Trowbridge's ice cream parlor in 1918. The plant and the ice cream parlor on Court Street were separated by a chilling tower. The business is listed as the Trowbridge Creamery Company at 316 North Court Street in the 1920–1921 city directory. Still open today, Trowbridge's is a downtown favorite. (FLPL.)

The Florence Wagon Works Company opened its doors in Florence in 1889, after the owner, Dr. A.D. Bellamy, relocated from Atlanta because of the cheap river transportation and inexpensive timber available in Florence. The company was extremely successful, and its wagons were widely distributed across the United States and to foreign countries. Because of the Florence Wagon Works' popularity, the phrase "Light Running Florence" became a household expression. Some wagons produced by the company even saw action in France during World War I. However, as automobiles began to replace horse-drawn transportation, orders for wagons gradually declined. Florence Wagon Works attempted to continue business as a manufacturer of lawn furniture, but the move came too late. The plant closed in 1941. Dr. A.D. Bellamy also established the Bellamy Planing Mill (below) on Union Avenue, near Sweetwater Creek. In 1905, Bellamy sold the mill to Andrew Marcus Lewellan. Lewellan changed the name of the mill to the Acme Lumber and Manufacturing Company. Lewellan ran the company until his death in 1924. (Both UNA.)

Since before the Civil War, many cotton mills have been located on the banks of the Tennessee River in Florence. The Globe Factory complex was located on Cypress Creek, and the creek was dammed to help provide power for its operations. In 1863, Union forces burned the mills. After the war, Cypress Mill was rebuilt; however, it was never very successful, and in 1889, interests in the mill were sold. Many of the workers moved to the Mountain Mill, which was located near Barton, Alabama. By 1893, the Mountain Mill Company had changed its name to the Cherry Cotton Mill in honor of its largest stockholder, Col. Noel Franklin Cherry, and moved back to Florence. The new mill was located on Sweetwater Creek. The mill grew quickly, reaching a capacity of 12,000 spindles and 400 employees in 1903. Employees were paid between 15¢ and 75¢ a day, depending on their position. The factory remained prosperous until the Great Depression hit Florence, when factory owners were forced to close its doors. (UNA.)

The Ashcraft Cotton Mill was located near the old Florence Canal and the Broadus Factory Reservation. The mill, owned by Cyrus W. Ashcraft, began operation in 1898 and remained in the Ashcraft family until 1918. The mill continued to operate until the end of World War II. (UNA.)

In 1902, the Chapin Ice and Coal Company united with the H.J. Moore Coal Company to become the Florence Ice and Coal Company. In 1903, the Florence Ice and Coal Company purchased land in East Florence on Aenta Street to construct a new ice factory. To make the ice, water from the Sweetwater area of Florence was pumped from a spring and purified and then frozen into large blocks. (UNA.)

This undated photograph shows the interior of the J.W. Stutts Drug Company in downtown Florence, probably at the turn of the 20th century. Like many early drugstores, the J.W. Stutts Drug Company acted as both pharmacy and restaurant, as can be seen by the immaculately polished lunch counter in the foreground of this image. (FLPL.)

This photograph of the interior of Young's Confectionery shows Virgil Young manning the counter of his mother's store. Generations of Florentines enjoyed patronizing Young's, and many Florence State Teachers College students frequented this establishment to grab a bite to eat between classes. (FLPL.)

The transition from horse-drawn transportation to motor vehicles was gradual in the Shoals. These photographs of M.T. Keller's blacksmith shop on Tombigbee Street in the early 1900s shows how blacksmith shops handled the transition. In the image above, Tom Keller (left) is in the process of working some fresh horseshoes, possibly for the team at right, while an automobile waiting for repairs is parked in the back of the shop. The image below shows Tom Poole in the foreground while Tom Keller stands in the far background. (Both FLPL.)

266 Hill Auto Company, located on the southwest corner of Huntsville Road and Royal Avenue, is said to have been the second service station in Florence. The owner, Fred Hill, also operated the Hill Cab Company from the service station. (UNA.)

In 1921, Richard Harvey Wilson and Ardell Stults opened Stults and Wilson Grocery on South Royal Avenue. In 1926, Wilson sold a pair of mules, a harness, and 25 bales of hay in order to raise $500 to buy out Ardell's share of the business, and the name was changed to the Wilson Food Center. (UNA.)

The Jefferson Hotel (above), located at the corner of Court and Tennessee Streets, behind the courthouse, opened its doors to the public on November 1, 1902. The building it occupied had been erected in the 1890s and served for a brief time as the city hall of Florence. A 1903 advertisement for the hotel said that it had "fifty rooms all furnished complete with antique oak finish furniture and white and gold metal beds fitted with perfection mattresses and downy pillows" and that it was "heated entirely by steam heat." This elaborate building was destroyed by fire in the early 1920s. In 1925, Charles Negley built his Negley Hotel on the site (below). (Both FLPL.)

Basil's Café was located on the corner of Court and College Streets in Florence. This image shows the café in the 1930s. (UNA.)

The iconic Italianate facade of the Southall Drugstore has loomed large in the skyline of Court Street since 1901. When construction of the building was first completed, it was considered by many to be one of the finest buildings in town. It was repurposed into living and office spaces in the early 1980s. (FMS.)

William H. Cromwell, a local druggist, owned W.H. Cromwell's Staple Groceries and Feed. He went on to purchase the Milner Drugstore in 1940, which is still a local fixture. (UNA.)

Feldman's 5¢ and 10¢ Store and Jackson Hardware, pictured here in the late 1920s, were located on the west side of Court Street, north of Mobile Street. (UNA.)

Clyde Anderson owned the Anderson News Company, pictured above in 1917. The newsstand stood on the corner of Court and Tennessee Streets and was originally constructed out of old piano crates. Anderson later purchased a bookstore. His sons went on to purchase other bookstores across the South. In 1964, they incorporated the stores under the name Bookland. Today, the chain, renamed Books-A-Million in 1992, is the second-largest bookstore chain in the country. The old Anderson Bookland location (below) in downtown Florence now operates as the headquarters for fashion designer Billy Reid. The new Books-A-Million store is located on Cox Creek Parkway. (Above, UNA; below, FMS.)

William L. Reeder had the Hotel Reeder built in 1917. Reeder was a director of both the First National Bank of Florence and the Florence Land Company. The hotel, located on Tennessee Street, contained 96 rooms. There was an annex containing 27 additional rooms. The hotel closed on October 20, 1967. (FLPL.)

Roger's Department Store began as the Surprise Store in 1894. The store, located at 117 North Court Street, was the first in North Alabama to have air-conditioning and elevators. The original building burned in 1910 but was rebuilt quickly that same year. In 1948, the building was renovated in the Art Deco/Moderne style. The building houses shops and offices today. (FMS.)

The Florence Shoe Company operated during a time when made-to-order clothing was the norm rather than the exception. This photograph shows the Florence Shoe Company, as it appeared in the 1930s, at its location on North Court Street. The company, which was owned by Lithuanian immigrant M.B. Israel, was in business on Court Street until 1962. (FLPL.)

Located next door to his Florence Shoe Company, M.B. Israel operated a dry goods store on Court Street for many years. This photograph shows Israel standing amidst his wares in 1919, the same year that he was naturalized as an American citizen. In addition to being a successful merchant, Israel was also a prominent member of Florence's local synagogue, Temple B'nai Israel. (FLPL.)

The small triangular piece of property where Wood and Morrison Avenues intersect in front of Wesleyan Hall was once a very busy place. Businessman Robert V. Stevens's Triangle Soda Bar, seen here in 1954, was an especially popular hangout for students of Florence State Teachers College, but its menu of hamburgers and soft drinks appealed to Florence residents of all ages. (FLPL.)

Before the triangular piece of property between Wood and Morrison Avenues was the Triangle Soda Bar, it was Young's Confectionery. Owned by Lula J. Young and built next door to her (now demolished) family home, Young's Confectionery—like the Triangle after it—catered to the appetites of Florence State Teachers College students. (FLPL.)

40

Peck Hardware, now Peck Ace Hardware, has been a fixture in Seven Points since 1927. Seven Points is located just north of the campus of UNA. The area was Florence's first suburban neighborhood and has its own downtown area. (FLPL.)

The Florence Opera House building, no longer standing, was located on East Tennessee Street. At the time of this picture, the space had been converted from theater space to offices and rooms for rent. (UNA.)

The East Florence Drugs building was constructed in 1889. Located at 1401 Huntsville Road, the structure sits in the East Florence Historic District. Charles A. Sullivan operated the first drugstore in the building on the first floor. A doctor's office occupied the second floor at one time. (UNA.)

The A&P Grocery store was located on North Court Street. (UNA.)

Louis and Anna Rosenbaum, with their son, Stanley, moved from Denver, Colorado, to the Shoals area in 1919. Louis had already embarked on a career in the movie theater business, having opened theaters in Douglas, Wyoming, and North Little Rock, Arkansas, before his arrival in Florence. During its heyday (1919–1939), famous personalities, including Gene Autry, Lash LaRue, W.C. Handy, and Fats Waller, performed at the Princess Theater, which was also an opera house. He went on to open eight other theaters through his company, Muscle Shoals Theaters, including the Shoals Theatre in Florence and the Colbert Theatre in Sheffield. Louis and Anna became pillars of the Shoals community and were well known for their charitable efforts. In 1937, Louis loaned money to the Florence United Methodist Church to prevent foreclosure on the building. Louis and his son, Stanley, also donated $40,000 to the city to help with the construction of the first public library in Florence. Louis and Stanley also helped to found a chapter of the Alabama Council on Human Relations, an organization that helped fight for racial equality. (UNA.)

In 1948, Louis Rosenbaum opened the Shoals Theatre. When the 1,350-seat theater was built, it was the fourth-largest theater in the state and featured state-of-the-art equipment. The theater, which has been restored and reopened by the Shoals Community Theatre Board, is located at the corner of Seminary and Mobile Streets. (UNA.)

Stagg's Grocery, an East Florence landmark since moving to what used to be the heart of the textile mill district in 1937, is still going strong. Originally, it was a mom-and-pop grocery store that fixed cold-cut lunch sandwiches for the mill workers on the side. Through the years, as the textile mills closed and larger grocery stores appeared, Stagg's Grocery's main focus moved from groceries to food service. The restaurant still operates today. (UNA.)

In 1902, Russell and Arthur Pratt began a Coca-Cola bottling franchise in Huntsville. They moved the franchise to Sheffield in 1906 and then to Florence in 1907. Initially, the plant was located at the corner of Wood Avenue and Tennessee Street. The company then moved to South Court Street. Pratt Bottling Company not only bottled Coca-Cola, but it also manufactured its own soda flavors and made ice cream. Russell Pratt left Florence in 1909 and went on to bottle and distribute Coca-Cola for the entire Pacific coast. Arthur Pratt left the Florence plant in the hands of Julia Pratt and her manager Burt Synder and went on to take over Coca-Cola distribution in Newark, New Jersey, and New York City. The Pratt Bottling Company was sold to Walter Matthews Sr. in 1940. Today, the Coca-Cola Bottling Company is located in the Florence Industrial Park. (UNA.)

Culpepper's Bakery was a staple of community life in Florence for many decades. Multiple generations of Shoals residents fondly recall Culpepper's as the best place in town to get pies, cakes, and pastries for every occasion. The bottom image shows Charles Olson making pie-crust shells in the Culpepper's Bakery kitchen in the 1960s. (Both FLPL.)

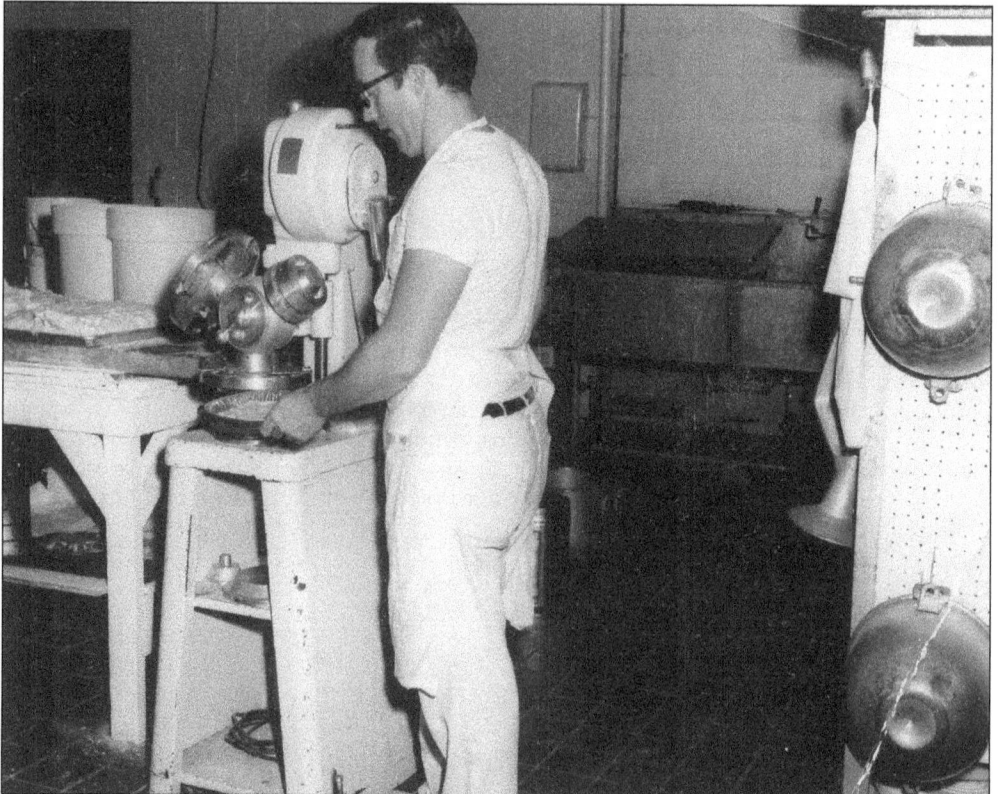

Abroms Department Store, seen here in 1935, was a fixture of Florence for generations. Closing its doors at 113 North Court Street after many years of downtown business, Abroms Department Store was a prime example of the late-20th-century trend of family-owned businesses being put out by national chain stores. (FLPL.)

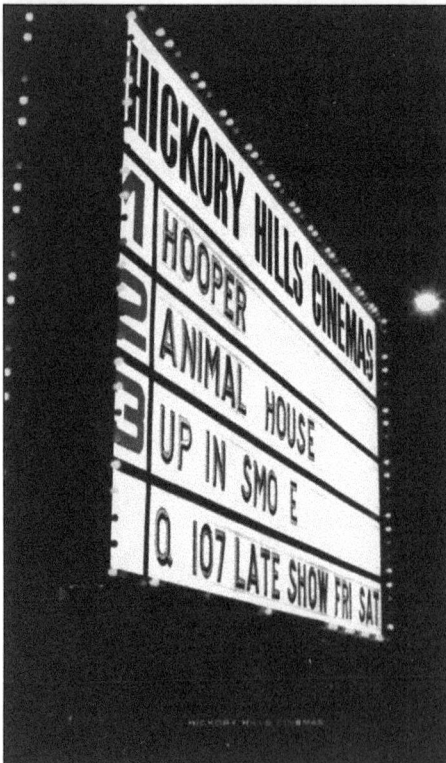

The Regency Square Mall opened in 1978 on Cox Creek Parkway. The same year, Hickory Hills Cinema opened with three screens on Florence Boulevard. The mall and the cinema represent a shift in Florence, a shift that was happening all across the country. New businesses increasingly were located on the edges of communities, rather than in the historic downtowns. Despite this shift of services away from the heart of the community, Florence's downtown remains vibrant today. (Both UNA.)

Three

HISTORIC HOMES

This home, of unknown date or ownership, is a good example of early vernacular architecture in Lauderdale County. The house is of the classic Dogtrot style, laid out with a large central hallway, which may have originally been a breezeway between two smaller cabins before being closed in to make a parlor. This type of vernacular architecture was probably of Appalachian origin and was common in the rural areas of North Alabama. (FLPL.)

This is an image of the home of Chief George Colbert (1764–1839), who was a leader of the Chickasaw Nation. Colbert was the son of a Scottish trader and a Chickasaw woman from a powerful family in the Chickasaw Nation. Because Chickasaw power was matrilineal, Colbert's mother's position ensured that his family would remain a dominant force in Chickasaw politics for generations. His biracial heritage also meant that he grew up bilingual, which made him and his brothers valuable assets to the tribe. The Colberts were the chief negotiators of the 1816 Chickasaw Cession to the United States, which opened Lauderdale County—as part of a huge 6,000,000-acre swath of territory—to white settlement. As can be seen here, his house was of vernacular European-American architecture. (FLPL.)

Located at 500 North Court Street, Rogers Hall is one of the most distinctive buildings in Florence. Courtview, as it was originally known, is a Neoclassical antebellum mansion. The home faces the north entrance to Court Street. In the 1850s, when prominent cotton planter George Washington Foster wanted to build the home, he had to obtain special permission from the state legislature because he wanted to place it in the center of a major thoroughfare. Permission was granted on the condition that "the beauty of the home justify the inconvenience caused the people of the city." The home remained in the Foster family until Alabama governor Emmet O'Neal purchased it in 1900. In the 1920s, Thomas Rogers Sr. purchased the home. In 1948, Florence State Teachers College (now UNA) purchased the home from the Rogers family. The house has undergone two major renovations since the university purchased it. (UNA.)

In 1843, John Simpson, a merchant in Florence, built the house now known as Coby Hall on the site of his former home. A classic antebellum brick house, with a six-column portico with entrances to the ground and first floors, the house was designed with a distinctive Flemish Bond brick pattern. During the Civil War, both the Union and Confederate armies occupied the residence. The Simpson family sold the house in 1867 to George W. Foster, the owner of Courtview, located just down the street from Coby Hall. Foster gave the house to his daughter Virginia and her husband, James B. Irvine. The house, then called Irvine Place, remained in the Irvine family for most of the 20th century. In 1990, David Brubaker gave the house as a gift to the University of North Alabama in memory of his wife, Coby Stockard Brubaker, hence the name, Coby Hall. (UNA.)

Built in 1820 by George Coulter, Mapleton, located at 420 South Pine Street, is an outstanding example of Federal-period architecture. The high level of the craftsmanship, as seen in the Adamesque woodwork around the interior doors, mantels, and partitions, is exceptional. George Coulter came to Florence from Kentucky, where he had been a planter and lawyer. He used slave labor to construct the house. In the mid-1850s the house was sold to George W. Foster, who bought the house for his daughter Virginia and her husband, James Irvine. After living in the house but a short time, the couple decided they would prefer to live closer to Virginia's parents, and Foster purchased the home now known as Coby Hall for them. Like many Florence homes, military forces occupied the house during the Civil War. Union troops, according to legend, hid their horses in the home's basement. (UNA.)

The Wood-Robinson house is an example of pre–Civil War architecture in Florence. Built in 1845, the home is one and a half stories, built around a central hall plan. The house has five bays and a gabled roof with chimneys at either end of the house. Victorian trim was added to the home in the late 19th century. (UNA.)

At the intersection of Waterloo Road and Savannah Highway sits Woodlawn. The Federal-style home was built between 1830 and 1832. During the Civil War, like many homes in Florence, both Union and Confederate forces occupied it. (UNA.)

The Governor O'Neal House, on Court Street, was home to two Alabama governors: Edward Asbury O'Neal (1818–1890) and Emmet O'Neal (1853–1922). The elder O'Neal attended LaGrange College. He was an attorney and judge and served as colonel of the 26th Alabama Infantry before serving as governor from 1882 to 1886. The younger O'Neal, also an attorney, grew up in the home and later lived in Courtview. He served as governor from 1911 to 1915. (UNA.)

On North Pine Street sits the Ashcraft-Dabney Home, an excellent example of Federal-style architecture. Built in 1831 or 1832, the brick home has a central pedimented portico, Ionic columns, and a Palladian window in the pediment. The house has an elaborate entrance, with fluted pilasters, sidelights, and a transom. The gable ends of the home display excellent examples of Federal-style chimney parapets. (UNA.)

"Father of Blues" W.C. Handy was born in this log cabin in Florence in 1873. Handy, who wrote such songs as "Memphis Blues" and "St. Louis Blues," was inspired by the music he heard African American residents of Florence sing as they worked in the fields and along the river. The cabin was moved from its original location in West Florence to its current site on West College Street and turned into a museum dedicated to Handy's life and music in 1973. (FLPL.)

Maryland native Benjamin F. Karsner and his wife, Sarah McCarter, built the Karsner-Kennedy House around 1828. This home is considered among the best examples of Federal-type cottage architecture and is one of the few remaining in the Southeast. Oscar and Bertha Carroll Kennedy later owned the house. The building is now the headquarters for Florence Main Street. (FLPL.)

Wakefield was one of the earliest brick homes in Florence. An exact replica of George Washington's ancestral home place (also named Wakefield), Wakefield was built around 1825 by Florence brick mason and contractor James Sample. The stepped chimneys, dentil work under the eaves, and the circular window woodwork are just a few examples of the exceptional craftsmanship evident at Wakefield. For many years, the home was owned by Rev. Dr. W.H. Mitchell, of the First Presbyterian Church, who was arrested by Union forces for praying publicly for the welfare of Confederate troops. (FLPL.)

While the date of Pope's Tavern's construction remains a mystery today, the building has played a large role in the history of Florence, stretching back to its earliest days. Located on Jackson's Military Road, which ran from Nashville to New Orleans, the building has served as an inn, a tavern, a hospital for the Confederate army, and a stagecoach stop. For many years, the Lambeth family owned the building and used it as a private residence. Currently, Pope's Tavern is part of the city of Florence's museum system. (Both UNA.)

Pickett Place is a relatively rare example of the "double-pile" (two-room-deep) Alabama Tidewater-type cottage. The Tidewater-type cottage style made its way from the Chesapeake Bay region to Alabama by the early 19th century. Thomas J. Crowe, owner of the National Hotel in Florence, built the home in 1833. It later became the home of Richard Oric Pickett, an attorney who arrived in Florence in 1843. Pickett was colonel of the 10th Alabama Infantry during the Civil War. (UNA.)

The Price Homestead is the oldest house on Walnut Street. Florence physician Dr. William M. Price built it in 1889. The home has a pressed tin roof and floor-to-ceiling windows on the front porch, rarely seen in other homes of the same period. The picture shows the home in 1900. The house has recently been restored to its original appearance by the current owners and is an excellent example of historic preservation done well. (Courtesy of Michelle Farris-Hyde.)

The Reisman-Coffee-Looft House (pictured above around 1890) and the Hall-Westmoreland-Colburn House (below) are excellent examples of Queen Anne architecture. The Queen Anne style reached the height of popularity during the 1880s and 1890s in Alabama and was very popular in industrial communities like Florence as a way to demonstrate newfound wealth and power. The houses also represented a homogenization of American architecture, with similar designs appearing all across the country thanks to popular magazines and the railroad. The Reisman-Coffee-Looft house's combination pyramidal and gabled roof and its weatherboard-and-shingle siding are common stylistic elements of the Queen Anne period. The Hall-Westmoreland-Colburn house has a multigabled roof and a square tower with a pyramidal roof—also common in Queen Anne homes. The houses are located in the Wood Avenue Historic District. (Both UNA.)

Another example of Queen Anne style, the Smith Home is also located on North Wood Avenue. Its combination gable and hipped roof, shingle-and-weatherboard siding, square and octagonal towers, roofline cresting, and a tin roof are all common elements of the Queen Anne style. (UNA.)

Thimbleton is located on West Tuscaloosa Street. The home is one of the few surviving examples of the Second Empire style in Alabama. Second Empire, which appeared in Alabama from the 1870s to the 1890s (after it had gone out of style in most other areas), was modeled after French Renaissance architectural styles. The mansard roof, seen here on Thimbleton, is the most noticeable feature of this architectural style. (UNA.)

Built by the Florence Lumber Company, the Ware-Wade House (1916) is one of the purest examples of the bungalow style in Florence. The home is one story with a full-width porch supported by rubble piers. The gabled roof has a shed-roof dormer, very common in bungalows. The style, first popularized in California, was radically different from the Queen Anne and Neoclassical styles that were so popular in Florence in the late 19th and early 20th centuries. (UNA.)

The Florence Lumber Company also built the Redd-Flippo House, located on North Poplar Street. The house was completed in 1917 and, like the Wade-Ware house, is an excellent example of the bungalow style and possesses exceptional examples of Craftsman-style workmanship. (FLPL.)

The A.D. Bellamy Place was located on the corner of Wood and Tuscaloosa Street. Dr. A.D. Bellamy, who owned the Bellamy Planing Mill (later Acme Lumber and Manufacturing Company) and was the founder of the Florence Wagon Works, relocated from Atlanta to Florence in 1889. (UNA.)

Moncure Woodson built the Camper-O'Neal House around 1890. Camper was a man who wore many hats. He was a native of Virginia, Confederate veteran, member of the Virginia State Legislature and mayor of Fincastle, Virginia. In Florence, he was an editor of the *Florence Herald* and founder in 1890 of the *Florence Times* (now the *Times Daily*). (FLPL.)

The Hicks family house was the residence of African American physician Dr. Leonard Jerry Hicks (1899–1973). Dr. Hicks came to Florence in the early 1930s. Despite rumors to the contrary, Hicks was not the first black physician in Florence. A half-dozen others preceded him in the late 1880s and early 1900s. However, Hicks was the first black physician to be elected to both the Lauderdale County Medical Society and the Alabama State Medical Society. (FLPL.)

James J. Douglass had the Kennedy-Douglass House built in 1918 on the site of an earlier frame house. Rev. Hiram Kennedy-Douglass of Trinity Episcopal Church continued to live in the house after his parents died. Elbert Bascome Wright, who bought the corner lot from James Douglass in 1904, built the Wright-Douglass Annex next door. (FLPL.)

Built in 1925, Lacefield is the best example of Dutch Colonial architecture in the shoals area. The home is a mixture of stone-and-stucco construction. The original owners, James and Estelle Lacefield, passed on the home to their daughter Marie Lacefield Shanks, who played a large role in the historic preservation movement in Florence. (FLPL.)

The Redd-Bibbee house was built by the Florence Lumber Company in the mid-1930s near the campus of UNA. The stone cottage, a product of the English Cottage Revival of the early 20th century, still contains much of the original interior woodwork and fixtures. (FMS.)

In 1939, Louis and Anna Rosenbaum celebrated the marriage of their son, Stanley, to Mildred Bookholtz of New York with a gift of a building lot and funds to build a house on Riverview Drive. Through the recommendation of one of their friends, Aaron Green, the Rosenbaums contacted Frank Lloyd Wright about designing a home for them. Wright's design for the Rosenbaum home is an excellent example of his Usonian style, an organic style of design in which the home seems to rise from the earth. The home was completed in August 1940. By 1947, the family had grown; the Rosenbaums had three sons and another on the way. They contacted Wright to design an addition for them, which was completed in 1948. The home, radically different from any other homes in Florence, became a centerpiece in the Florence community. The Rosenbaums' home was also an intellectual and cultural gathering place in Florence. The Rosenbaums actively supported the Civil Rights movement and were extremely involved in their community—supporting the Florence Lauderdale Public Library, the Florence Concert Association, and the Temple B'nai Israel. (FLPL.)

Four

FARMS AND PLANTATIONS

One of the major motivations for settlement across Alabama in the early 1800s was the area's rich farmland. Soil in the eastern part of the country had been depleted and farmers sought new lands for crops, especially cotton. The need for better land led to treaties with the Chickasaws and Cherokee who lived in the Shoals region and opened the Shoals for settlement in the late 1810s. (UNA.)

Before the Civil War, Florence had some of the earliest cotton mills in North Alabama. After the war, it took Florence a bit to recover, but as production began anew in the 1880s and 1890s, the Tri-Cities (Florence, Sheffield, and Tuscumbia) began to play a larger role in the region's cotton economy. This image shows the area around the courthouse, which served as a market for cotton farmers from all over Lauderdale County. (FLPL.)

In the early 20th century, agriculture across Alabama began to diversify, partially as the result of the extension service. Beef, poultry, and forestry products began to replace some of the cotton lands as total reliance on cotton became more and more precarious. (UNA.)

Across much of the country after World War I, crop prices began to fall. By the time the Great Depression hit Alabama, the amount of acreage under cultivation had dropped dramatically. New techniques, machines, and fertilizers also made it possible to produce more on fewer acres. The Shoals region was one of the major centers of fertilizer production in the United States. During World War I, in 1917, President Wilson chose Muscle Shoals as the site of two nitrate plants to be used for national defense. A dam would also be built to generate the necessary power to the plants. When the war ended less than a year later, the plants sat idle. When TVA entered into the picture in 1933, the plants began to produce fertilizer, which TVA distributed through county soil-conservation agencies. The fertilizers and increased mechanization radically changed the landscape of the Tennessee Valley region and other areas across the country, as they improved the nutrient content of the soil and allowed farmers to double their production rate per acre. (Both UNA.)

The Forks of Cypress was once the crown jewel of an immense plantation. This Greek Revival home was built in 1830 and featured a two-story colonnade that consisted of 24 Ionic columns, one of the only early homes in the state of Alabama to have this feature. It was the home of wealthy horse-breeder, state representative, and Irish immigrant James Jackson, who was also an early investor in the Cypress Creek Land Company. Many racehorses today can trace their bloodlines back to Florence and the three horses Jackson imported to the Forks of Cypress from England in the 1830s: Leviathan, Gallapade, and Glencoe. The building was a hub of social activity in the antebellum era, and remained a center of community activity until a lightning-induced fire destroyed it in 1966. The Forks of Cypress gained national attention as the setting of the Alex Haley book *Queen*, and its accompanying television miniseries, in the 1990s. (Above, FLPL; below, UNA.)

John Brahan built Sweetwater Plantation between the years of 1828 and 1835. Brahan received around 4,000 acres of land in Florence for his service in the War of 1812. It was called Sweetwater Plantation because at the foot of the hill upon which the mansion was built there was a spring called *succataina* by Native Americans, meaning "sweetwater." John Brahan died before the completion of the house, and his daughter Jane Brahan Patton, wife of Robert Patton, inherited the estate. During the Civil War, both Federal and Confederate troops camped on Sweetwater Plantation. In 1863, Federal soldiers raided the plantation and robbed the Patton family. Robert Patton went on to become the 20th governor of Alabama in 1865. In 1885, Robert Patton died, and the plantation was passed to Col. John Weeden and his wife, Martha Hayes Patton Weeden. Martha Patton Weeden was the daughter of Governor Patton. (UNA.)

In 1952, Dr. Kirk and Lillian Deibert purchased close to 90 acres at what is now the corner of Cox Creek Parkway and Darby. They came to Florence from Nashville, where Dr. Deibert had taught radiology at Vanderbilt University. Dr. Deibert was the first board-certified radiologist in the Shoals. (FLPL.)

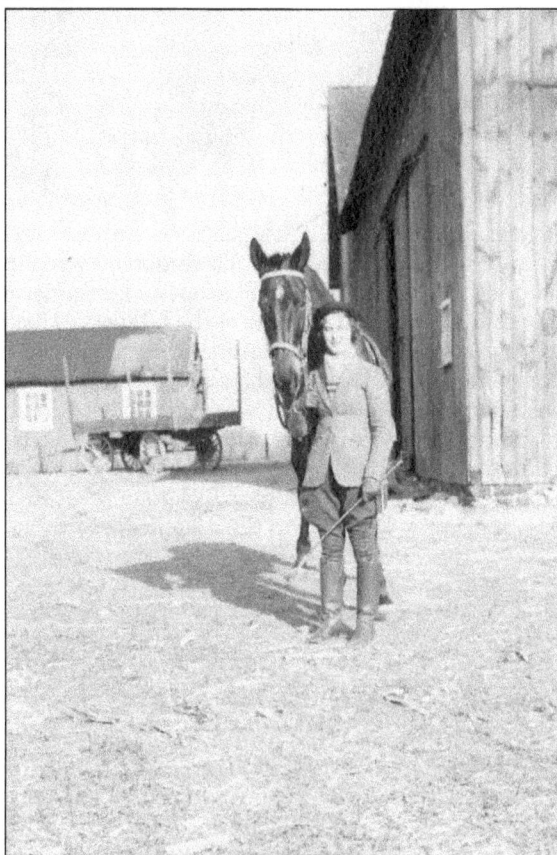

Lillian, who grew up in Haddonfield, New Jersey, loved horses from an early age. She learned to ride from her uncle Clarence. When Kirk and Lillian purchased the 90 acres of land in Florence, Lillian began to build up her own herd of horses while also running the day-to-day operations of the farm. (FLPL.)

Initially, Lillian faced difficulties farming the Deibert property. The land was extremely worn out from over-farming, and it took two years of intense fertilization and cover crops to begin to establish pasture for the horses. (FLPL.)

Lillian also initially faced difficulties because in running the farm, she violated gender norms of the time. As she put it, she had problems finding farmhands "because no one wanted to work for a woman farmer." Eventually, she managed to find some workers who accepted that she, not her husband, was in charge of the day-to-day operations of the farm. (FLPL.)

Lillian taught riding lessons to community members while also showing her horses. Kirk also rode. (FLPL.)

In 1991, tragedy struck the Deibert family: a fire started in the horse barn. The fire destroyed the barn and killed their 27 Arabian horses. The family was devastated by the loss and buried the horses on their property. Before Kirk's death in 1993, the Deibert family made the decision to donate their property to the people of Florence to be used as a passive park instead of selling it to developers. On May 25, 2000, Deibert Park was dedicated. The park has walking trails, playgrounds, ponds, and is home to the Children's Museum of the Shoals. (FLPL.)

Five

EDUCATION

Founded on January 11, 1830, a few miles south of Leighton, Alabama, as a nondenominational college, LaGrange College was the first state-chartered college in Alabama. In 1855, college president Dr. R.H. Rivers moved the school to Florence and reincorporated the school as Florence Wesleyan University. In 1863, the Union army burned the community of LaGrange and the original school buildings. (UNA.)

Designed by Adolphus Heiman and built by Zebulon Pike Morrison, Wesleyan Hall was completed in 1856 for Florence Wesleyan University. The building represents one of the few surviving examples of public Gothic Revival architecture in the Tennessee River valley region. It features a crenellated parapet and octagonal towers mark each corner of the building. When it first opened, the building contained all of the classrooms and administrative offices for Florence Wesleyan University. Wesleyan Hall was occupied by both Union and Confederate troops during the Civil War. The building is still a central part of the campus of the University of North Alabama. (Both UNA.)

In 1871, Florence Wesleyan University closed its doors and the school was reopened as the State Normal School in 1873. It was the first normal school south of the Ohio River. Normal schools were designed to provide training for teachers. Women were admitted in 1874, making the State Normal School the first coeducational institution of its type. The institution functioned as a normal school for more than 50 years. This image, taken in 1923, shows the students and faculty of the State Normal School. (UNA.)

Construction began on Bibb Graves Hall in 1929 on the campus of the newly renamed Florence State Teachers College (previously, the State Normal School). The building, designed to house the administration of the college, as well as classrooms, the college library, and a science lab, was built in the Gothic Revival style already prevalent on campus. Named for Alabama governor Bibb Graves, Bibb Graves Hall is one of many public buildings in Alabama named after Graves, known as the "education governor." The building opened in 1930. (Both UNA.)

Completed in 1934, the Memorial Amphitheater has been the site of many special events on the campus of the University of North Alabama, including graduation celebrations and dramatic presentations. The 10 Doric columns and the entablature of the Memorial Amphitheater represent the traditional style of design and construction of amphitheaters stretching back to ancient Greece. (Both UNA.)

Willingham Hall was built on the site of the former Locust Dell Academy, a girls' school run by Nicholas and Caroline Hentz from 1834 to 1843. The building, a WPA project, began as a dormitory for men in 1939. In 1947, the building became a female dorm after the construction of Keller Hall and remained so until 1969, when it transitioned into housing office space. Today, the English, history and political science, and criminal justice departments have offices in the building. The building was named for State Normal College president Henry Willingham (1913–1938). (FLPL.)

When Bibb Graves opened in the 1930s, it held the university library, as shown here. In 1940, a new library was built, replacing the library in Bibb Graves. In 1949, the new library was named to honor Dr. C.B. Collier who served as dean of Florence State Teachers College from 1918 to 1946. (UNA.)

This image shows a Florence State Teachers College class going on a field trip with its teacher, Susan Price. Such events were one of the few situations where women were allowed to wear pants or shorts on campus. Susan Price was a faculty member in the geography department from the late 1890s to the 1930s and served as secretary of the State Normal School Alumni Association. (UNA.)

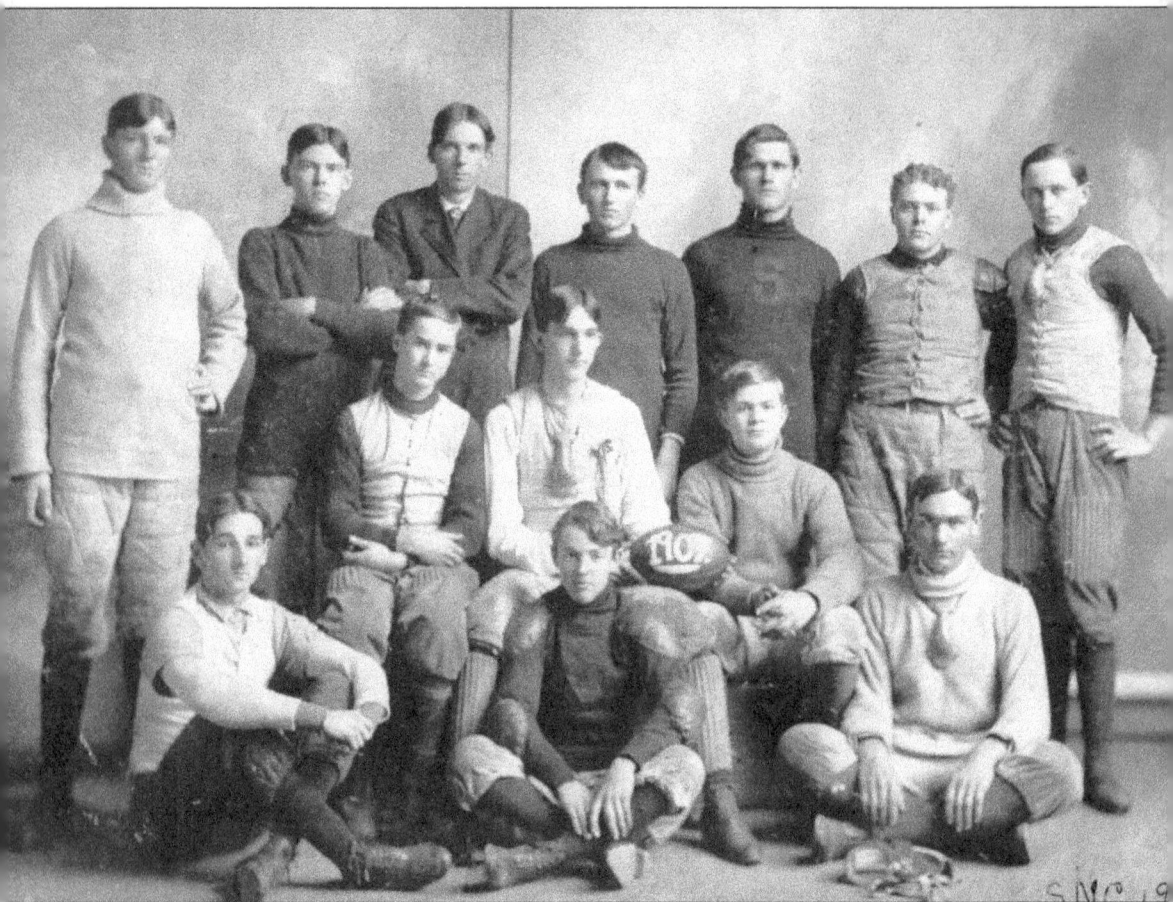

In 1906, the first athletic associations are noted in the catalog of the State Normal College, with "official" college football and baseball teams first mentioned in 1911. The football team struggled during its early years (including a rather embarrassing 101-0 loss to Sewanee: The University of the South in 1912) and the school abandoned the sport in 1928 after losing its only two games of the season. Football did not return to the college in 1949, and by then, the school had been renamed Florence State Teachers College. In 1907, the State Normal College football team consisted of 13 players. Pictured are, from left to right, (first row) K. O'Neal, E. Darby, and F. Burns; (second row) R. Mitchell, L. Deprez, and J. Ewin; (third row) W. Anderson, H. Algood, B. Beddingfield, L. Guin, T. Lemdy, A. Simpson, and P. Keller. The team went 3-2 in 1907. (UNA.)

This image shows 1906 State Normal College baseball team. (UNA.)

This image shows the 1913 State Normal College football team. (UNA.)

As a way to provide teacher training, the State Normal School opened the Model Training School, which has developed into the present-day Kilby School. In 1922, during the tenure of Gov. Thomas K. Kilby, a building for the newly renamed Kilby School was constructed just west of Wesleyan Hall. This building housed the first six grades, while the high school classes continued meeting in the two buildings used for college classes at the State Normal School. This arrangement continued until 1929, when the institution became Florence State Teachers College. That year, the college adopted a four-year curriculum for students majoring in elementary education and Kilby School was restructured to include only grades one through eight. In 1950, the seventh and eighth grade were eliminated. (Both UNA.)

Kilby School moved to a new structure west of Pine Street in 1964. A kindergarten program was added to the school in 1970, and in 1975, a nursery school was built adjacent to the main school. The school retains close ties to the University of North Alabama and still provides training opportunities to students in the department of education. (UNA.)

In 1833, Nicholas and Caroline Hentz established Locust Dell Academy in Florence for female students. Hentz was a painter, entomologist, and author and had been the chair of modern languages at the University of North Carolina. Caroline Hentz wrote plays, poems, short stories, and novels. The Hentz family left Florence in 1843, but Locust Dell Academy continued to operate until it was absorbed by Florence Synodical Female College in 1855. (UNA.)

Theophilus B. Larimore, seen here at work on his back porch, was the founder and first principal of Mars Hill Bible School. Larimore and his wife, Esther, founded the Mars Hill Academy in 1871 on 27 acres of land outside of Florence. Although the school closed in 1888 to allow Larimore more time to focus on his ministerial work, it was reopened in 1947 and continues to exist today as Mars Hill Bible School. (FLPL.)

In 1847, the Florence Female Academy opened its doors. However, it struggled financially, even after a $20,000 contribution by the City of Florence, and was forced to shut its doors. In 1855, the academy property was absorbed by the Florence Synodical Female College, which had been founded by the Presbyterian Synod of Nashville. Zebulon Pike Morrison, who would also build Wesleyan Hall, constructed the two buildings that housed the academy. The school trained young, genteel women in languages, drawing, painting, music, English, geography, and arithmetic. The school remained open until 1893, and in 1895, the property was sold to pay debts. In 1911, the dormitory building was torn down to make room for the new Florence Post Office. The educational building remained standing until 1972. (Both UNA.)

In 1889, the Florence Educational Land Development Company was formed with the goal of creating a Baptist university in Florence that would be able to compete for students with some of the South's best institutions, including Vanderbilt University. Dr. J.B. Hawthorne, a prominent and well-known Baptist minister, played an instrumental role in the founding and building of the school, initially named Hawthorne College. However, in 1891, the administrators of Hawthorne College accepted an invitation from Dr. H.M. Caldwell to move to Birmingham and occupy the former Lakeview Hotel Building. The building in Florence sat empty for 16 years. In 1908, the building reopened as the Florence University for Women. Unfortunately, the building burned to the ground on March 2, 1911, due to faulty wiring. Luckily, no one was injured in the fire. (UNA.)

The Patton Elementary School was built in 1890 on land given to the city of Florence by Gov. Robert M. Patton. The school was originally designed to serve all of the white elementary school children in Florence. The building also housed the Florence superintendent's offices. Ada Coffee, a leading Alabama educator, joined the faculty in 1896 and served as principal from 1910 to 1944. Coffee was dedicated to improving the school's physical structure, opening the first school lunchroom, and in 1921, under Coffee's direction, the third floor of the school was removed. Additionally, Coffee oversaw the installation of safety doors and fire escapes. She also established the first parent-teacher association. In 1958, when the African American high school in Florence burned, the white students moved from the Patton School to the J.W. Powell School and about 360 African American junior and senior high school students used the Patton building from January 5, 1959, until the new African American Burrell-Slater High School building was completed in 1960. The Patton School building was then torn down. (UNA.)

The Brandon Elementary School, located in the Sixth and Seventh Wards in the eastern portion of Florence, opened in 1899. Charles M. Brandon, a partial owner of the Florence Wagon Company, donated the land on which the school was built. (UNA.)

In 1891, the Fifth Ward School was established on North Wood Avenue in a three-room building. In 1921, land was purchased along Sherrod Avenue and Gilbert Court in order to build a new school (shown here). The name of the school was changed to the Gilbert School, in honor of H.C. Gilbert, who had served as superintendent from 1892 until 1904. (UNA.)

The Weeden Heights School, located in present-day East Florence, was built in 1919. The school was named for John D. Weeden, who was the grandson of Alabama governor Robert M. Patton. The Weeden Heights School originally was located in two frame structures, one for first-graders and the second for students in second through sixth grades. The current school was built in 1955. (UNA.)

Founded in the 1820s by Jonathan Bailey, the Bailey Springs Resort was located just outside of Florence on County Road 47. From 1893 to 1900, there was a female university, Bailey Springs University, located at the resort site. (UNA.)

Patton School was established on Hough Road in Florence, on land carved from the Sweetwater Plantation of Gov. Robert Patton. Not to be confused with the larger R.M. Patton School, this facility was much smaller and was known locally as the Patton/Weeden school. This image shows the school's pupils in 1910. (FLPL.)

Coffee High School, named for Capt. Alexander Donelson Coffee and his wife, Camilla Madding Coffee, opened in September 1917, replacing the Florence High School, which was located in an antebellum home on North Pine Street. The school was located on the corner of Hermitage Drive (then Jackson Highway) and Nellie Avenue. In 1951, a new high school was built on North Cherry Street. The former Coffee High School building became an elementary school and was renamed F.T. Appleby School. Fire damage led to the school being torn down in the 1980s. (UNA.)

Fire drills are an important rite of passage for America's schoolchildren, as well as an essential practice to keep everyone safe. The Florence Fire Department has a rich heritage of cooperation with the city's public school system, as can be seen in this photograph taken by Florence Firemen at a fire drill in Appleby Junior High, probably in the late 1950s. (FLPL.)

Six

HOUSES OF WORSHIP

This image from the 1940s shows a mass baptism in one of the many lakes around Florence. Such mass baptisms were a frequent occurrence in the Shoals region through much of the 19th and 20th centuries. (UNA.)

Located at 224 East Mobile Street, the First Presbyterian Church is the oldest continually operating congregation in Florence. Organized in 1818, the first sanctuary was built in 1824, and in 1830, James A. Sloss was installed as the first permanent minister. During the Civil War, its minister, the Rev. William H. Mitchell, was pulled from the pulpit and arrested by Union soldiers under the command of Union colonel and future Supreme Court Justice John Marshall Harlan. What was Mitchell's crime? He was praying publicly for Confederate president Jefferson Davis, his cabinet, the Confederate Congress, and the success of the Confederate armies during the Sunday service at First Presbyterian. Mitchell spent the next three months in a Union prison camp in Illinois before some influential friends secured his release. The church buildings have undergone several major renovations and expansions, first in 1898, following a fire in 1927, in 1957, and in 1968. (FLPL.)

Trinity Church and Rectory, Florence, Alabama 1911.

Now located at the intersection of Tuscaloosa and Pine Street, Trinity Episcopal was organized in 1836 by the Rev. Thomas Armstrong Cook at the southwest corner of College and Cedar Streets. The Rt. Rev. Nicholas Hamner Cobbs consecrated the church on February 23, 1845. After fire damage in 1893, Trinity was relocated to the present site in 1894. The first worship service was held on Easter 1895. The Rt. Rev. Richard Hooker Wilmer consecrated the new church on June 12, 1898. The bell from the original church hangs in the current church. The Parish House was added in 1929. The Mullen Hall and educational building were erected in 1967. (Both UNA.)

First Baptist Church of Florence was organized in 1888 and baptized new members in Cypress Creek. In 1889, the Lauderdale County Baptists Association, the church's first missionary effort, was organized. By 1903, the church was fundraising to support a missionary in China. They held worship services at the Lauderdale County Courthouse until 1890, when the congregation constructed a rudimentary wooden structure at the corner of Walnut and Tombigbee Streets. The first sanctuary burned in 1909, and in its place, the congregation built the Neoclassical brick building seen here. Today, First Baptist occupies all of the surrounding city block, but its second church building continues to serve the congregation as the chapel. (UNA.)

Started as a mission of First Baptist Church of Florence, the church began in 1896 as an outreach to the factory workers of East Florence. The mission was constituted as East Florence Baptist Church in 1900 and changed its name to Central Baptist Church in 1919. The new house of worship was built in 1923 at the corner of Huntsville Road and Aetna Street. (UNA.)

The First United Methodist Church was organized in 1822. The church met first in the log home of its minister, Rev. John Cox. In 1826, the first dedicated sanctuary was erected on the present site of the church. That building was replaced by a larger structure in 1902, pictured above, which stood until it was destroyed by fire in 1920. The current sanctuary, pictured below, was finished in 1924. During the construction of the current sanctuary, the congregation met for worship at the old Coffee High School building. During the Great Depression, the church had an outstanding mortgage that it could not pay due to the financial constraints of the congregation. Local Jewish philanthropist and businessman Louis Rosenbaum intervened and wrote a check to the congregation that kept its doors open. (Both FLPL.)

Poplar Street Church of Christ was one of the first Church of Christ congregations in Florence. Organized in 1886, its early congregants included T.B. Larimore, who founded Mars Hill Bible School. The congregation met in members' homes until the structure pictured above was built in 1890. The congregation held services in this building until moving to Wood Avenue in 1970, and it changed its name to Wood Avenue Church of Christ. The new church, pictured below, is located on the corner of Wood Avenue and Tuscaloosa Street. Master masons the Putman brothers, who also constructed the First Christian Church on North Wood Avenue, built the church, which, despite its modern appearance, owes much to the Gothic tradition in church architecture. (Above, FLPL; below, FMS.)

Liberty Baptist Church, near the intersection of County Road 8 and the Natchez Trace Parkway, was organized in 1852, making it the oldest existing Baptist congregation in Lauderdale County, and, until the formation of First Baptist Church of Florence in 1888, the only Baptist congregation in the county. This picture is of the original wooden sanctuary, which was used by the congregation until 1892, when a brick structure was built to take its place. As can be seen here, the church had two doors—one to be used by men and one to be used by women. Seating in the church was segregated by sexes, with a special section for senior deacons. (FLPL.)

In the spring of 1904, the East Florence Free Will Baptist Church bought property at the corner of Mill Avenue and Sweetwater Avenue to build a church. In September 1944, the church relocated to the corner of Stevenson Street and Sweetwater Avenue. In 1964, the church moved to the present location on Highway 72, and the first service was held on May 1, 1966. (UNA.)

The Calvary Fellowship Church was originally built in 1890 as Poplar Street Christian Church (now Wood Avenue Church of Christ) by Florence contractor A.P Holtsford, who was also a member and a Church of Christ minister. The Church of Christ moved out of the building in 1970, at which time the building became the home of the nondenominational Calvary Fellowship Church. (FLPL.)

Members from First Baptist and Central Baptist Churches in Florence founded Highland Baptist Church on October 12, 1924, at 215 Simpson Street. Rev. J.L. Ivey was the first pastor. The original building was destroyed by fire on Sunday, December 14, 1941. Construction on the new building began on June 2, 1942, and was officially dedicated on January 10, 1943. The newest sanctuary was completed just a few years ago. (FLPL.)

The cornerstone for the Bethel Cumberland Presbyterian Church was laid on November 25, 1897. Construction of the current building, pictured here, began in 1920 under the leadership of Rev. O.R. Stephens. Renovations have taken place twice—once in 1941 and again in 1996. Had the 1996 renovations not taken place when they did, it is likely the church's west wall would have collapsed. (FMS.)

St. Joseph Catholic Church was built atop Lawton Heights. Rev. Fr. Benedict Menges, OSB, reported in the *Florence Gazette* of June 4, 1878, his intention of founding a Catholic church and school in Florence. A frame building was constructed during the missionary pastorate (1883–1889) of Rev. Fr. Polycarp Scherer, OSB, of Our Lady of the Sacred Heart in Tuscumbia (founded in 1869). The present building was completed in 1974. (FLPL.)

The Eastside Church of Christ can trace its roots to the late 1920s when the first African American Church of Christ congregation was formed in Florence. The congregation has moved locations in Florence multiple times. Its most recent location on East Tombigbee Street originally was built in 1947 to house the First Church of Nazarene. The Eastside Church of Christ purchased the building in 2004. (FMS.)

St. Marks Missionary Baptist Church is located at 220 East Alabama Street. An African American Baptist congregation has continuously used the site of the current church since 1859. The original "church" began as a brush arbor before being replaced by a frame structure during the tenure of Rev. Cordey White. This frame structure was then replaced by the current structure in 1901. (FMS.)

First Christian Church had its start in 1917 in an old skating rink on Court Street. In early 1918, the congregation purchased a home at the corner of Tuscaloosa and Walnut Streets, and after a fire in 1922, members built a church on the site. It was not until Easter Sunday 1950 that the congregation moved to this building across from the campus of the University of North Alabama. (FMS.)

The congregation of Our Redeemer Lutheran Church, officially organized in 1938, met in Florence City Hall until 1940. The dedication of the new building on North Poplar Street, shown here, took place on December 8, 1940. As the church has grown, the congregation has made an excellent effort to match the new additions to the original design. (FMS.)

While there had been Jewish residents residing in the Shoals since the mid-1800s, Temple B'Nai Israel was not incorporated by the State of Alabama until 1906. The temple was to serve Jewish residents from Sheffield, Tuscumbia, and Florence. The original building was in Sheffield. The building pictured here was constructed in 1956 on East Hawthorne Street in Florence. (FLPL.)

Seven

PEOPLE

Construction of Wilson Dam began in 1918 and lasted until 1925. The project employed more than 18,000 workers, many of whom traveled across the river to Florence occasionally. This image shows workmen arriving in Florence from Muscle Shoals. They are standing in front of Milner's Drugstore, which opened in Florence in 1853. The store chain, now Milner-Rushing Pharmacy, is the oldest continually operating pharmacy in Alabama. (UNA.)

In the final days of the Civil War, emboldened by the absence of law and order, several groups of paramilitary desperados preyed on the populace of Lauderdale County. One of the most notorious gangs was led by "Mountain" Tom Clark. Clark's gang of Union deserters committed several heinous murders, rapes, and acts of plunder. Clark himself confessed that he had killed 18 people and one child. He was captured in September 1874 by the man pictured here, city marshal William Edward Blair (1847–1894). Before he could be executed, a mob of local citizens broke into the jail by night and lynched Clark and two members of his gang in downtown Florence. Although local lore states that Clark was buried beneath Tennessee Street after locals recalled that he boasted that no one would ever "run over" him, extant documents from the case indicate that the three men were buried in a field nearby. (FLPL.)

This photograph from the late 1910s shows four Lauderdale County sheriffs gathered together. Their names and years of service are, from left to right, Joe Hines (1894–1898), O.B. Hill (1902–1908), Jess A. Dowdy (1908–1912), and Cal Young (1912–1916). (FLPL.)

This photograph is of William Jackson. William was the son of James Jackson, the Irish immigrant and breeder of racehorses who built the Forks of Cypress. (FLPL.)

One of Florence's most beloved law enforcement officers was chief of police Samuel Weakley Lipscomb (1857–1941). Chief Lipscomb was the first chief of police in Florence's history to be known by that title; all previous heads of law enforcement in the city had been known as city marshals or constables. Lipscomb served as chief of police in Florence from 1897 to 1901, conducting his patrols on bicycle. (FLPL.)

Florence Wagon Works, as the second largest wagon manufacturers in the nation (after Studebaker), employed 175 people at its peak. Pictured here are some of the Florence Wagon Works employees at the turn of the 20th century. (FLPL.)

In the early days of fire prevention, Florence's fire department was composed of volunteers who operated horse-drawn water pumps. This photograph shows the Florence Volunteer Fire Department at the turn of the 20th century, posing at the corner of Pine and Tennessee Streets. (FLPL.)

Although the late 20th century saw a spike in the popularity of football among Southerners, baseball was once the sport of choice for Shoals residents. In the early 20th century, many local businesses created baseball teams and held tournaments for employees. This photograph shows the Ashcraft Cotton Mills baseball team at the turn of the 20th century. (FLPL.)

The Pratt Bottling Company, which distributed Coca-Cola products from Florence, used the Tennessee River to ship products westward to Waterloo and Savannah, Tennessee. However, because of Muscle Shoals, they used wagons, like the ones pictured here, to ship Coca-Cola over land to the east end of Lauderdale County. (UNA.)

Col. George H. Nixon was a prominent citizen in nearby Lawrence County, Tennessee. As a veteran of the Mexican War with command experience, Nixon was quickly promoted to command of the Confederate 48th Tennessee Infantry when the Civil War began. His men fought in most of the major campaigns of the Army of Tennessee, and his command included many men from Florence and Lauderdale County. This image is of a reunion of veterans of Nixon's 48th Tennessee Infantry, around 1910. (FLPL.)

This image shows T.B. Larimore, the founder of the Mars Hill Bible School, enjoying watermelon with family and friends. (FLPL.)

In 1907, Florence built a new fire department building on Royal Avenue. This photograph shows the Florence firefighters on April 15, 1917. At the time, Donald White was the chief of the Florence Fire Department. (UNA.)

Florence Fire Department chief Donald White drove the Buick Roadster seen here in a photograph from 1928. (FLPL.)

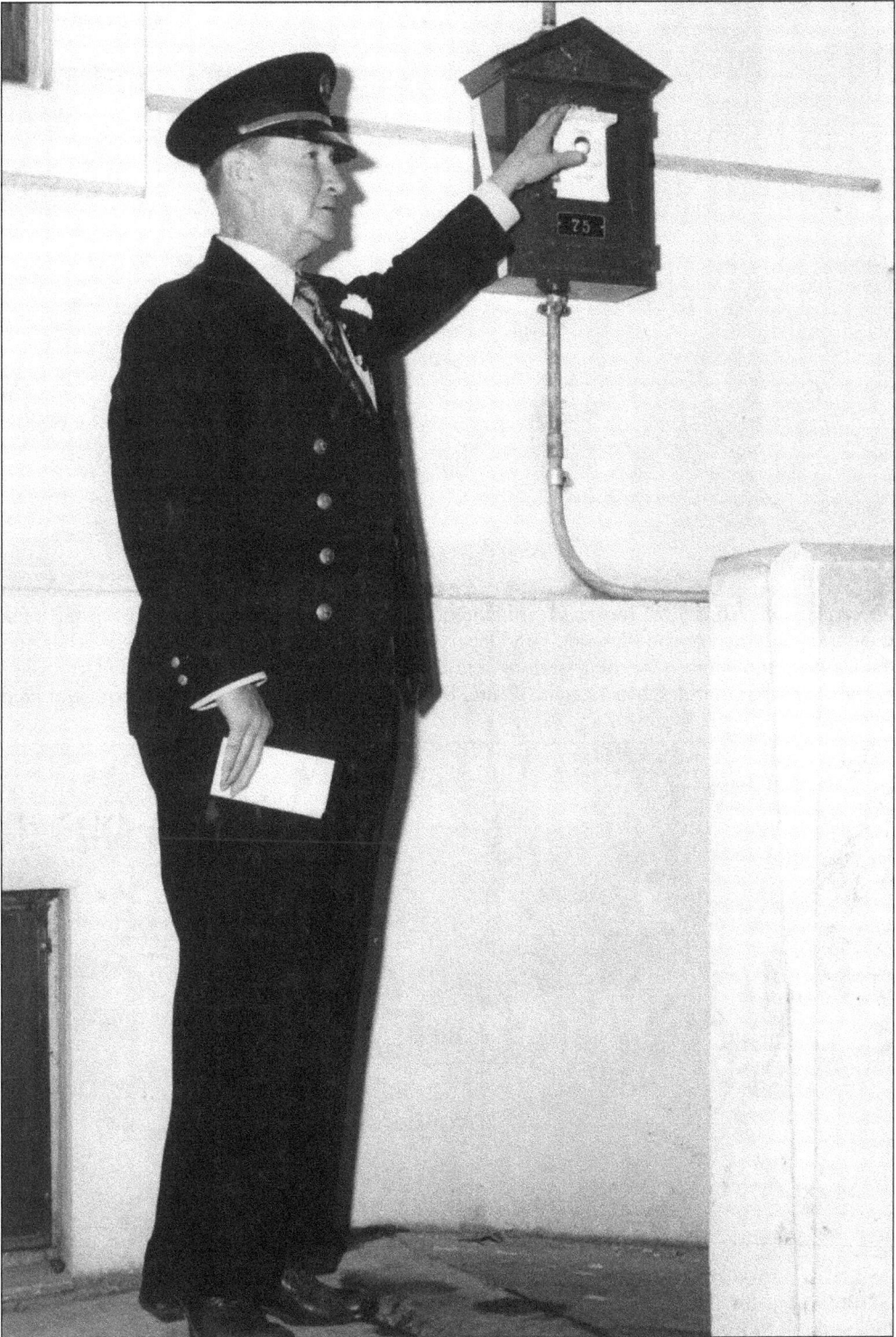

In this undated photograph, a uniformed Florence fireman activates the alarm that alerted all on-duty firemen to take their posts in order to respond to an emergency. (FLPL.)

On January 8, 1926, a snowstorm buffeted Florence and left the region blanketed in white. Some industrious firemen of the Florence Fire Department took advantage of the cold weather and built a large snowman near their station. The firemen in this picture are identified, from left to right, as Al Stanford, Chief Donald White, Bill Snyder, W.C. Taylor, M.H. Guerro, and Fred Fago. (FLPL.)

As well as being a vital economic resource for Florence, the Tennessee River is also an important cultural asset. Since earliest times, the river has teemed with fish, mussels, and other aquatic life, making fishing a prolific recreational activity for many Lauderdale County natives. This pre–World War II image shows a group of friends trying their luck in one of the county's many fish-rich creeks. (FLPL.)

The Great Depression hit the Tennessee Valley especially hard. Destructive farming methods, outdated infrastructure, and crushing poverty had plagued this part of the South since the Reconstruction era. When banks failed in the late 1920s, it meant that many Shoals residents were living under what would now be considered third-world conditions. Franklin D. Roosevelt's New Deal program placed a special emphasis on modernizing and rehabilitating the Tennessee Valley with the creation of the Tennessee Valley Authority, which he headquartered in nearby Muscle Shoals. This is an image of the president as he traveled through Florence to the ceremonies officially opening TVA in 1933. (FLPL.)

Many Shoals men answered the call to arms when the United States entered into World War II. This photograph shows native son James C. Faulkner posing with his motorcycle after entering the US Army during that period. (FLPL.)

Before the era of artificial Christmas trees or modern Christmas lights, one of the top risks of holiday house fires was the Christmas tree. In an effort to combat these holiday house fires, one of the Florence Fire Department's annual Christmas traditions in the mid-20th century was tree dipping. Cosponsored by the Lions Club, tree dipping involved submerging Christmas trees in a flame-retardant liquid to reduce the chance of holiday house fires. (FLPL.)

When the Florence Fire Department is not fighting fires, it seeks out other ways to serve the community, as can be seen in this photograph of a bicycle safety session at Florence Fire Department Station No. 3 in October 1950. Firemen applied safety tape to children's bicycles to ensure that they could be seen at night. (FLPL.)

To commemorate FDR's visit to Muscle Shoals to open the Tennessee Valley Authority in 1933, John F. Kennedy paid a visit to the TVA facilities near Florence in 1963, on the 30th anniversary of the authority's founding. According to the *Florence Herald*, President Kennedy praised the enormous positive economic impact that TVA continued to have on the region, and defended the federal government's involvement in the project, saying that "the people of this area know that the federal government is not a stranger or an enemy, it is the people of 50 states joined in a national effort to seek progress in every state." (FLPL.)

This image shows (from left to right) George Lyles, Adrin Owens, and Preston Lewis walking in downtown Florence during the mid-1950s.

The Florence Fire Department prefers to train in situations that are as realistic as possible. As seen in this photograph from 1975, it has a long history of using condemned buildings for controlled-fire training simulations. (FLPL.)

This great pair of images shows the same four friends. The image above was taken in 1913 when (from left to right) Ruth Stuber Jearme, Meta Korn, Mrs. Ingram, and Mrs. Duncan were students at the Florence Normal School. The image below was taken 47 years later, in 1960. (FLPL.)

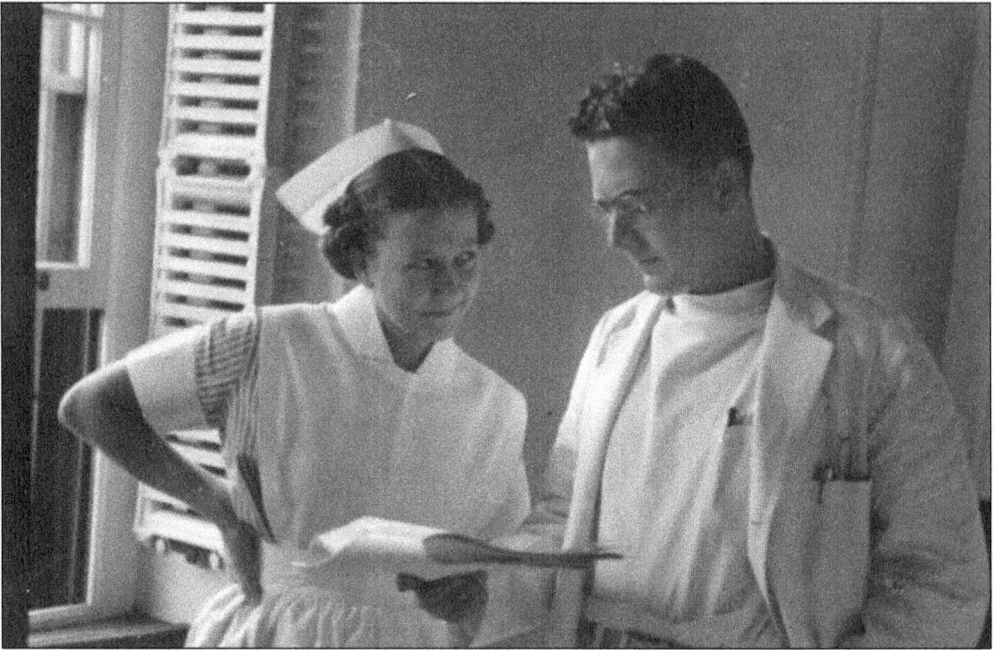

This image shows Dr. Kirk Deibert and nurse Hershey examining paper work. (FLPL.)

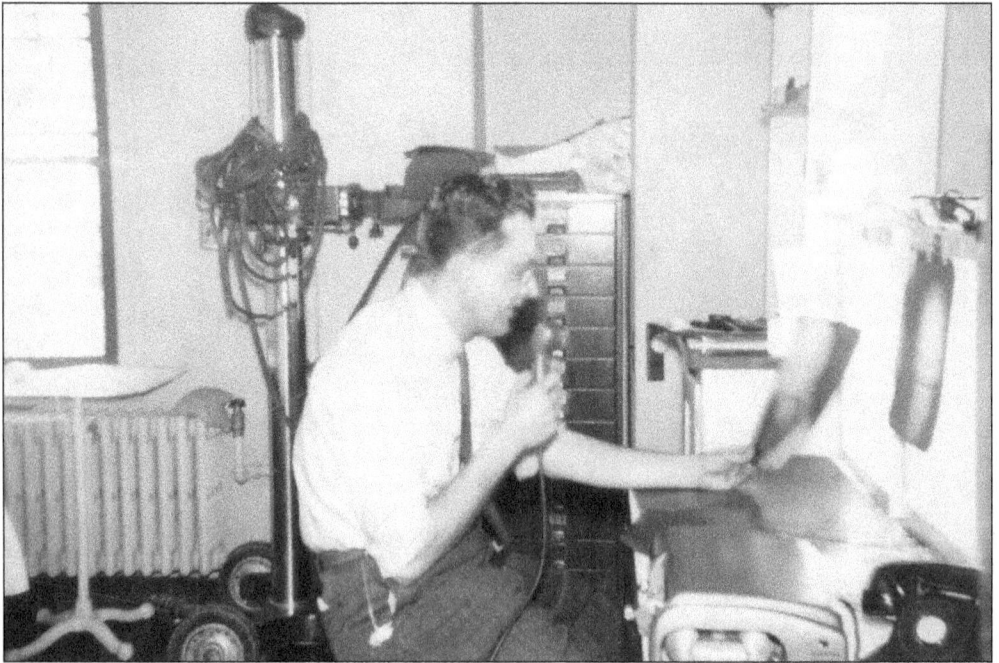

This photograph of Dr. Kirk Deibert reading X-rays was taken at the Eliza Coffee Memorial Hospital in 1955. (FLPL.)

BIBLIOGRAPHY

Alabama's Tapestry of Historic Places: An Inventory. Montgomery, AL: Alabama Historical Commission, 1978.

Broach, Barbara. *Frank Lloyd Wright's Rosenbaum Home: The Birth and Rebirth of an American Treasure.* San Francisco, CA: Pomegranate, 2006.

Gamble, Robert. *Historic Architecture in Alabama: A Guide to Styles and Types, 1810–1930.* Tuscaloosa, AL: The University of Alabama Press, 1990.

Garrett, Jill Knight. *A History of Florence with 1850 Census.* Columbia, TN, 1968.

———. *A History of Lauderdale County, Alabama.* Columbia, TN: 1964.

Hamm, Jane Johnson. *Florence Wagon Co.: Memories and More.* Florence, AL: 1997.

The Lauderdale County Heritage Book Committee. *The Heritage of Lauderdale County, Alabama.* Clanton, AL: Heritage Publishing Consultants, Inc., 1999.

McDaniel, Mary Jane, ed. *Historic Muscle Shoals: Buildings and Sites.* Manchester, IN: The Tennessee Valley Historical Society, 1983.

McDonald, William Lindsey. *A Walk Through the Past—People and Places of Florence Lauderdale.* Florence, AL: Blue Water Publications, 2003.

———. *Beginnings of the University of North Alabama: The Story of Florence Wesleyan University.* Birmingham, AL: Birmingham Printing and Publishing Co., 1991.

———. *Civil War Tales of the Tennessee Valley.* Killen, AL: Heart of Dixie Publishing, 2003.

———. *Lore of the River . . . the Shoals of Long Ago.* Florence, AL: Blue Water Publishing, 2007.

———. *Remembering Sweetwater—The Mansions, The Mills, The People.* Florence, AL: Blue Water Publishing, 2002.

———. *Sweetwater: The Story of East Florence, 1818–1940.* Florence, AL: Florence Historical Board, 1989.

Steen, Robert. *History of the Foster Home—Courtview—Rogers Hall and Early City of Florence on the Campus of the University of North Alabama.* Florence, AL: The University of North Alabama, 2007.

Tennessee Valley Historical Society. *Journal of Muscle Shoals History* Vols. 1–18.

Wallace, Harry. "History of the Shoals." *Times Daily,* February 25, 1999.

Visit us at
arcadiapublishing.com

www.ingramcontent.com/pod-product-compliance
Lightning Source LLC
Chambersburg PA
CBHW080632110426
42813CB00006B/1665